Exploration and Discovery

# The Computer Revolution

Author: David Jeremiah

Series Editor: John Becklake

**M**
MACMILLAN CHILDREN'S BOOKS
LONDON

# Contents

Left: Here are two pieces of equipment designed to help people count. In the background is an abacus. For many thousands of years people used these beads for counting. At the front is a modern circuit that uses electronics to count.

# The world of electronics

The story of electronics began in the early 1900s. Since that time many important developments have taken place which have brought electronics into our homes, our schools and our work places. The use of electronic equipment affects us all at some time in our lives. When you turn on a radio or a television you are using electronic equipment.

In most electronic equipment there is a small item called a transistor, which uses very little power. This means that we can use portable radios and televisions which rely only on power from a battery. Record players, tape-recorders, hi-fi and video all depend on electronics as well. In many schools we use 'closed-circuit' television and even computers to help us learn.

Telephone and telex machines, used to send messages all over the world, rely on electronics. The traffic light systems in our cities, and the complicated method of air-traffic control at our airports are all electronically controlled. In hospitals, doctors can use electronic equipment to listen to a baby's heart before it is born. When an X-ray is taken, the machine may be controlled by electronics. Clearly, electronics has had and is having a great effect on our world.

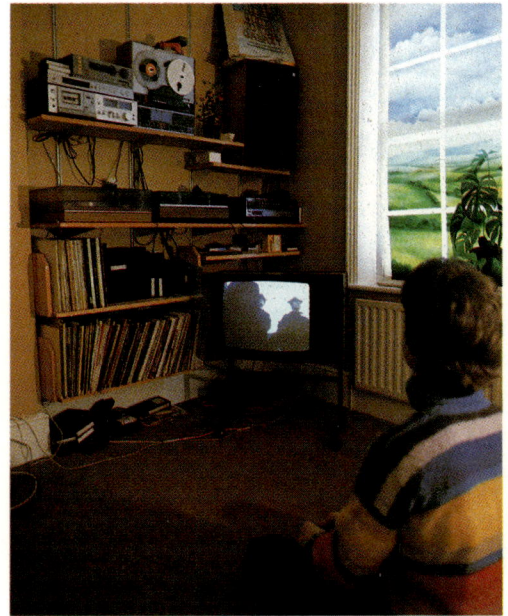

Above: Electronic equipment has become commonplace in our homes. Without it, there would be no television, radio or hi-fi.

Below: This girl is using a 'Visual Display Unit' (VDU terminal) at home.

These two pictures show how air travel has come to depend upon electronics. On the ground, radar is being used to show where aircraft are in the sky. Air-traffic controllers use radios to talk to the crew in the aircraft.

Electronic equipment in aircraft can pick up signals from ground stations. It then works out exactly where the aircraft is. In bad weather and at night, automatic landing equipment can help the pilot to land the plane safely.

Electronic detectors in aircraft tell the pilot that everything is working correctly. The use of electronics makes air travel much safer.

Until recently, cars had no electronics in their controls. Nowadays, many cars use electronic ignition to start the engine. This has several advantages: for example, the car is easier to start on cold, damp mornings and it should use less petrol. It is quite likely that, in order to save money, more cars will be fitted with electronic ignition as petrol prices keep rising.

The amount of petrol a car uses is also affected by other things, such as tyre pressure and oil temperature. To get the greatest number of kilometres to the litre, everything must be properly controlled. The development of very small electronic computers, called 'microcomputers', helps to do this.

Below: These are the pieces of equipment needed for electronic ignition. They replace the distributor which used moving parts to start the car. With electronic ignition there are fewer moving parts and the system is more reliable. Electronic ignition helps the car to do many more kilometres to the litre. It also reduces air pollution from the exhaust fumes of the car.

Inset: This is one of the first cars to be fitted with a microcomputer. This checks almost everything in the car.

# Valves and transistors

The world of electronics began when scientists first studied the flow of electricity in a circuit. They found that the electric current could be controlled by valves. These early valves were large and expensive to use. In the late 1940s scientists discovered that tiny pieces of the material germanium, when specially prepared, could do the same job. The development of these tiny 'transistors' was the beginning of miniature electronics. In 1958, a way was found to put more than one transistor on a piece of germanium. This was the first integrated circuit.

Nowadays, integrated circuits are usually made on another material called silicon. These silicon 'chips' can hold hundreds of thousands of components. These include transistors and also other things used in electronic circuits like resistors and capacitors.

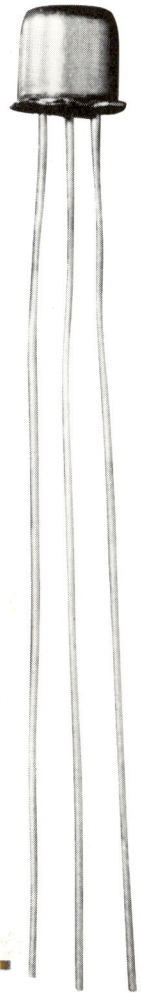

Top left: The valve was at one time an important component used in the control of current flowing through a circuit. Circuits using such components were used in early radios, televisions and gramophones. The circuits required quite a large amount of power, and a lot of space as you can see in the picture on the left.

Top right: The development of the transistor changed the world of electronics. The picture above is of a transistorized television. The transistors are capable of doing everything the valve could do, but the circuit takes up much less space.

7

# Simple machines that 'think'

One of the major benefits of electronic circuits is the speed at which they can work. For example, the 'signals' received by a radio are converted into sounds almost at once. Modern circuits on chips work far more quickly than older ones using valves or transistors. Nowadays, very complicated circuits can operate in millionths of a second.

This speed has proved particularly useful in the design of calculators. The electronics in a calculator work very fast. When two numbers are added or subtracted, the sum is done almost immediately. The result is then displayed. Multiplication and division are treated in the same way, because in a calculator, multiplication is treated as a series of additions, while division is treated as a series of subtractions.

People take far longer to feed the numbers into the calculator and to read the answer than the calculator takes to do even the most complicated sums. It is now quite usual to find calculators which can do complicated mathematical work and produce the answers at the press of a button.

Electronics has created a revolution in entertainment. Advanced circuits and microcomputers are used in exciting games which test the skill of the player. Games like Space Invaders are usually the most popular today.

## ADDING MACHINES

Calculators are probably the most common way in which we use electronics. Modern calculators can do very complicated sums at the push of a button.

The first calculators were not so complicated. The abacus was the earliest kind of adding machine. On the left is a mechanical calculator. On the right is an early form of transistorized electronic calculator, which can do calculations much faster.

Right: The spread of games like Space Invaders has not been restricted to amusement arcades and cafés. Because the equipment needed to play these games is so small and cheap to produce, it can be used to provide games at home. A great advantage is that the display used for these games is a television monitor. By plugging the equipment into the television at home, a whole range of games can be played.

Above: The use of electronics is likely to spread into other areas of entertainment. Because electronic circuits are so small nowadays they can be put in tiny items like this toy car. The signals transmitted from the control box can be 'interpreted' by the electronics, so that the car will work in the way the person operating it wishes.

The circuits in a calculator are special ones. They have been designed for a particular purpose. Other circuits can be designed to do different things. For example, a circuit could be designed to control the rate of flow of water through a pipe.

These special circuits must have ways of sending and receiving information. In most cases, the information or signal coming into a circuit (the 'input') will need to be changed before it can be used. When the circuit sends out a signal (the 'output'), this must also be translated into a usable form. So modern integrated circuits are usually accompanied by two other circuits – the input and output circuits which will do all the necessary translation of information. The integrated circuit combined with the input and output circuits mean that we can use electronic equipment to do some very difficult jobs.

Electronic equipment can receive input, send output and carry out complicated processes. This might give the impression that the equipment can think and make decisions for itself. The more complicated they are, the more it seems that these machines are 'intelligent'. This is not the case. The circuits are designed by people, and they can only do what people have 'told' them to do – no more and no less.

9

# The first computers

A computer may be described as a piece of equipment which is capable of storing and carrying out a set of instructions. These instructions are called programs. The computer should also be able to deal with different programs, which most simple calculators cannot do. It is this ability to carry out many different programs using the same equipment which makes computers different from other electronic equipment.

The idea of a computer is not new. The abacus – a counting-frame – is a simple calculator, and the first step along the road. Charles Babbage designed and began to build a calculating machine in 1822. This was an attempt to create an automatic mechanical calculator. However, it was not until valve circuits had been developed that the development of an automatic electronic computer was made possible.

Above: Is this the first computer? These Chinese children are using abacuses, or counting-frames. The abacus cannot store and carry out different programs, so it is not really a computer. However, an abacus can do various calculations.

Left: In the early nineteenth century, Charles Babbage aimed to develop a calculator which would use wheels and which would be powered by steam. The precision required was too great for the engineers of that time, and his 'analytic engine' never progressed beyond this experimental model.

Right: The first electronic computer in Europe was developed by Manchester University in the 1940s. It used valves and was very large.

# Electronic computers

Early valve computers were large and used a lot of power. They needed a lot of attention as the components were liable to break down often. When transistors began to be used, computers became smaller and used less power. But because each component was still an individual item which had to be wired into the circuits, the computers were still difficult to look after.

The development of integrated circuits made computers even smaller, and they required far less power. Because the whole circuits were designed and built as a single item, they were more reliable. The cost of production was also greatly reduced. If something goes wrong, engineers can replace a whole circuit without wasting too much time or money.

These developments have continued with what is known as 'large-scale integration'. Up to 100,000 components have been packed together on one chip of silicon. More recently, 'very large-scale integration' is being used. This allows up to 250,000 components on one chip of silicon. Computers have been used for many years in education and industry, now that they are small and cheap, they are becoming available to more and more people.

The development of transistors meant that smaller computers could be made which used less power. Even then, they were still large. This engineer is working on the first transistorized computer used in Britain known as the 'Cadet'. Each component of such a computer is soldered into place. This means that there is a high chance of circuit failure.

DESIGN COMPUTERS
Left: Modern computers may be small, like this desk-top model, but they can work out many difficult problems. For example, they are often used by engineers for design work. The computer displays a colour picture of the design on a screen like a television. Computers now help engineers to design such things as buildings and cars.

Right: This image was produced by a computer. It shows the space shuttle and its temperature on re-entry into the Earth's atmosphere. The engineers and scientists can make alterations to the design, and then display the space shuttle again to see if there are any changes in the temperatures.

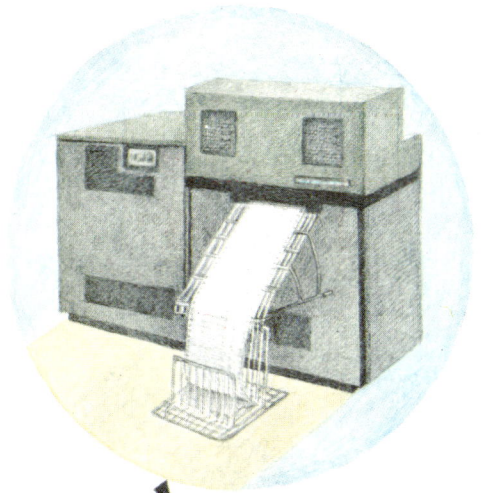

## A MULTI-USER SYSTEM

When many people can use a computer at the same time, the computer is called a multi-user system. Here is one such system. This is a police computer, which records the movements of the police. As soon as police officers have any information, they can put it into the computer, which will then store it until it is needed.

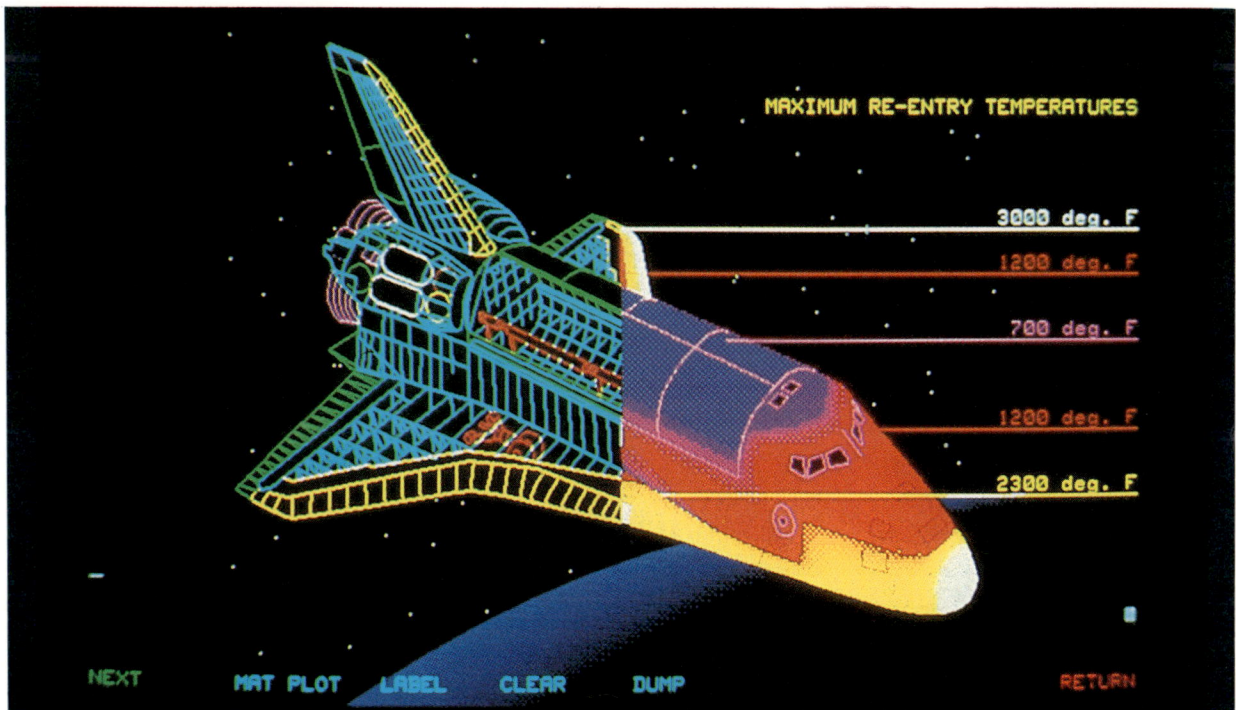

MAXIMUM RE-ENTRY TEMPERATURES

3000 deg. F

1200 deg. F

700 deg. F

1200 deg. F

2300 deg. F

NEXT          MAT PLOT   LABEL    CLEAR    DUMP                    RETURN

# What is a chip?

The idea of many components linked together on a single unit was first developed in the late 1950s. Chips were then called 'integrated circuits'.

Why 'chip'? The term refers to the small wafer or thin slice of silicon upon which the integrated circuits are built. Modern chips are very small. You could put 20 on a small postage stamp. On each chip there are thousands of parts. The first integrated circuit, on the other hand, contained only a few parts.

The method used to make chips have developed very quickly and it is now possible to put more and more complicated circuits on one chip. This made the microprocessor possible, and the microprocessor led in turn to the making of a very small computer – the microcomputer.

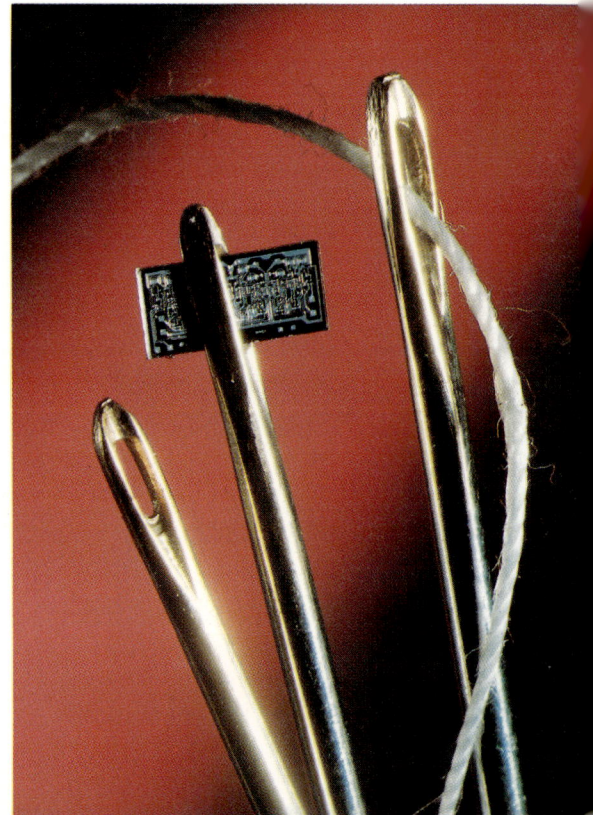

Right: This integrated circuit, made in 1968, was small enough to pass through the eye of a needle.

Below: This circuit is being designed by a computer. It will be transferred to a chip later.

The manufacture of integrated circuits is a complicated process. The need for cleanliness at all times is vital. Any dirt or grease interferes with the circuit-building – a speck of dust looks like a boulder under the microscope!

The production of a chip begins with a very pure piece of silicon, which is 10 centimetres across. A circular wafer of the silicon is cut from it. Many chips will be made from each wafer. The first layer of the circuit is cut into the silicon, and a 'dopant' is introduced. The 'dopant' is a chemical element which combines with the silicon and enables the individual components to be created. By repeating this process many times, the circuits are slowly built up.

Once the chip is completed, each circuit on the wafer is tested. Although many will fail, there are so many circuits produced that the number which pass the test will be high.

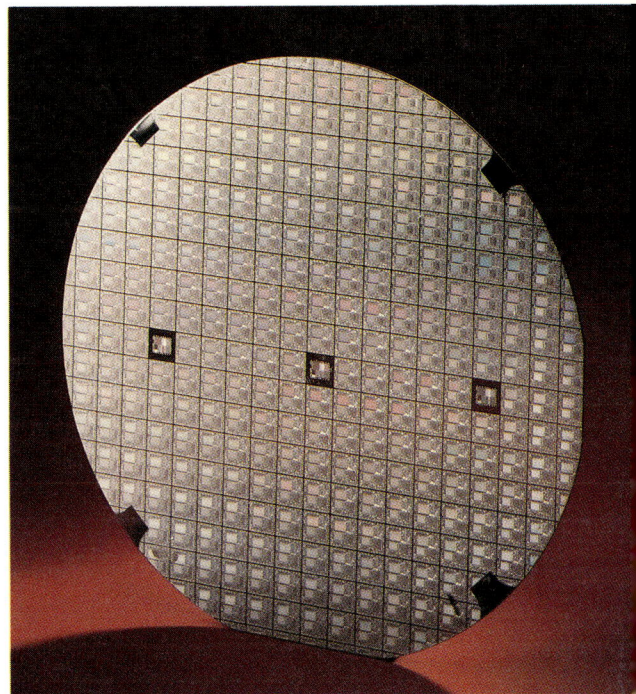

Above: This wafer contains over 250 complete integrated circuits which are ready for testing and cutting.

Many silicon wafers are prepared in one 'batch'. Cleanliness is vital; workers must wear special clothes.

# Microprocessors

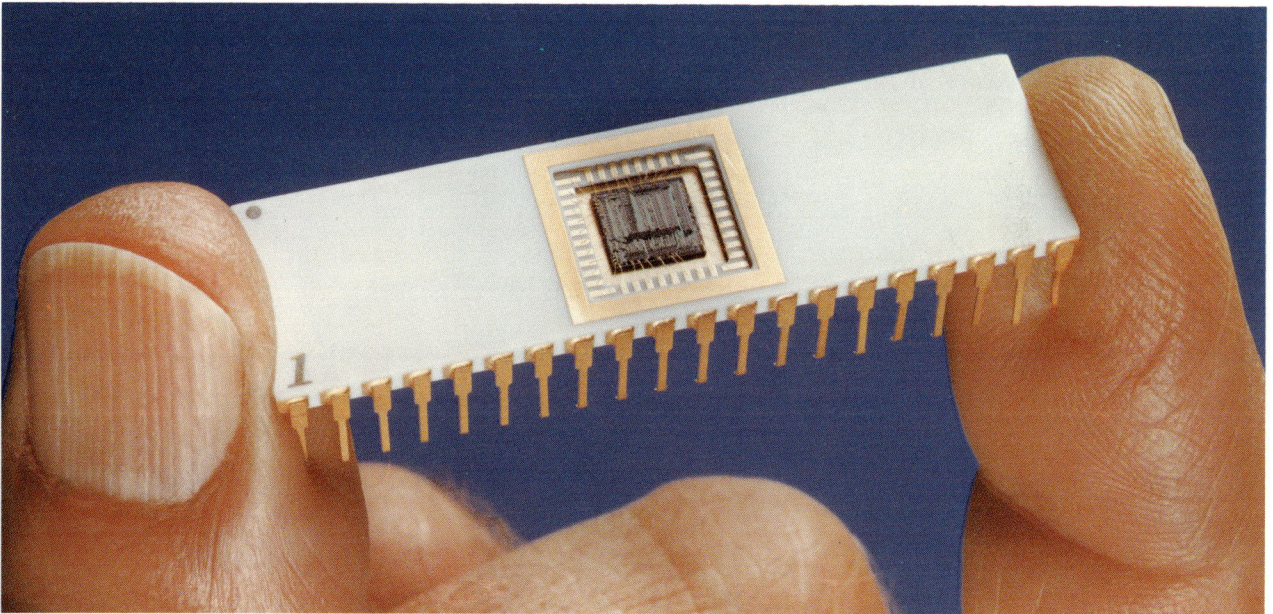

Microprocessors are really just complicated integrated circuits. They can be added to other circuits to make microcomputers. For instance, one circuit allows information to go in and out of the computer, and another remembers it. All these circuits can be combined on one chip or may be on several integrated circuits as a 'multichip' microcomputer.

All integrated circuits do a series of tasks automatically and might be said to be programmed. The program is normally built into the circuit and cannot be changed. With the design of a microprocessor, it is possible to tell the circuit to carry out a set of instructions. The set of instructions or 'program' can be changed when necessary to do different tasks.

This ability to be programmed is the most important aspect of an integrated circuit in a microprocessor. It means that the microprocessor can be 'told' to do different things and that it is not limited to doing just one specific task. However, because it has no memory, the microprocessor is not yet a computer.

Above: This is a microprocessor ready for use. The chip is fixed in the middle and is only ten millimetres square. The pins on the case containing the chip are used for the input and output of signals. These operate the microprocessor and are connected to the chip by thin gold wire.

Below: These two circuits do the same thing: they count. The one on the left uses just two integrated circuits. The first one actually does the counting. The second one decodes the signals of the first, and works the display unit.

Left: The electronics industry makes great use of integrated circuits and microprocessors. This board has many integrated circuits itself, and is used to test one particular type of integrated circuit – microprocessors.

Below: a computer is being programmed through a terminal.

Microcomputers have 'memory' circuits. These memories usually store instructions which the microprocessor must follow when carrying out a task.

There are several different types of memory. Random Access Memory (RAM) is used when the information is going to be changed from time to time. Read Only Memory (ROM) is memory which has the instructions built into it during manufacture. These instructions cannot be changed. Programmable Read Only Memory (PROM) is rather like ROM, except that the instructions are added after manufacture. All three types of memory can be used in a microcomputer.

Nowadays, it is cheaper to produce calculators by using a standard mass-produced microprocessor, with a ROM attached. Computer terminals may have microprocessors controlled by a PROM, and a RAM will be used when the microcomputer is employed for research in developing programs.

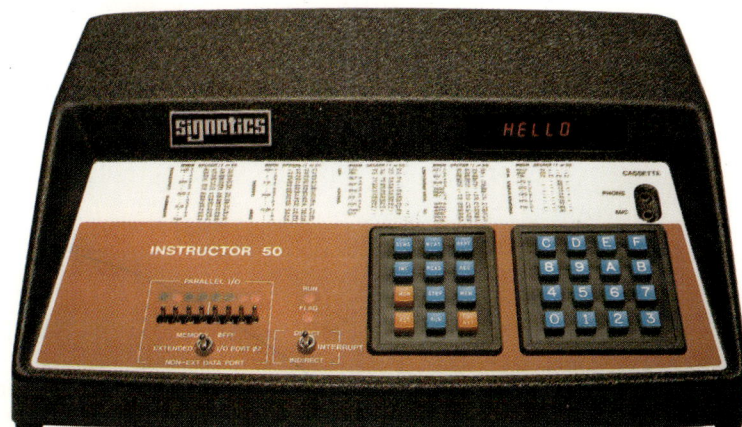

Left: This particular system is used to help teach people how to program microprocessors. Inside are the microprocessor and the memory units, as well as circuits which sort out the programmer's instructions. These instructions are put in by keyboard or tape-recorder. Another circuit controls the display screen. 17

# Chips in the home

Electronic equipment is widely used in the home nowadays. Radios, televisions and hi-fi systems have been familiar sights for many years. But micro-electronics, making use of microprocessors, has now provided us with digital watches, calculators, television games and many other gadgets. Soon they will be in common use in washing-machines, cookers and heating equipment. By using these circuits we can make control systems smaller. What does the future hold in store? We may use microprocessors to control the central heating or close the curtains to help save energy.

This washing-machine looks like an ordinary one, but it is special because it is controlled by a microprocessor circuit. The control unit carefully sets the water temperature, the timing and the kind of wash to give the best possible performance and economy.

Above: Microelectronics are also making a big difference in the world of communications. Push button telephones are becoming common now, and they represent the first use of microelectronic circuits in the telephone handset.

Right: Prestel is a combination of three items of equipment. Its purpose is to provide up-to-date information in your living-room. A special television displays information which it receives over a telephone line. The other end of the line is connected to a computer. With this type of system you can order shopping without leaving your home.

18

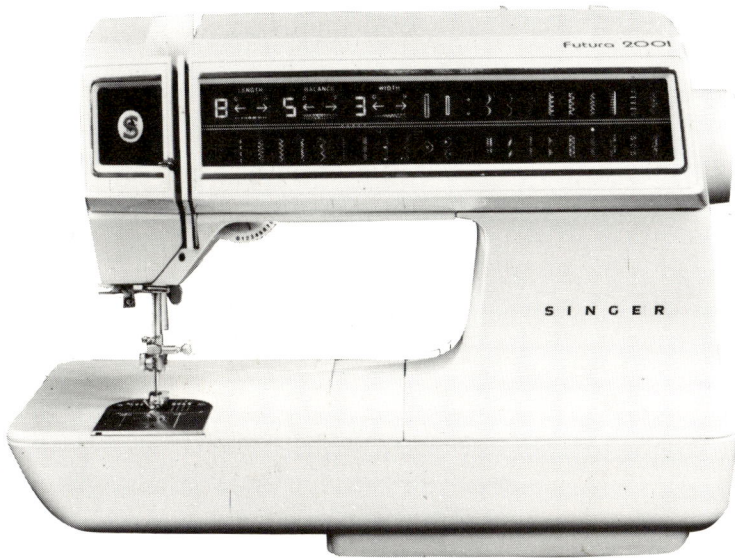

Above: Microprocessors are used in sewing machines. The machines will automatically sew the correct stitch again and again.

A microprocessor in your cooker means no more burnt meals – the cooking is timed exactly. Thanks to sensitive detectors, the oven temperature is kept steady.

Below: Microprocessors and chips make photography easy. The modern camera will automatically choose the right exposure and shutter speed.

# Education and research

Computers have been used in education and research for many years, but in the past there were only a few large computer systems, in universities and big research centres. However, with the development of microcomputers, more and more small computers are being used in schools and laboratories.

In schools, these computers help children to learn a particular subject, or are used by children to learn about the computers themselves. In laboratories, microcomputers help with experiments. They can be used to collect and analyse results, or control the experiments.

In the future, schools may change, so that children can learn their lessons at home with the help of a microcomputer. Each pupil will be able to learn at the speed which suits them.

Microcomputers can also be used to help handicapped people to learn and communicate. Microcomputer-controlled equipment needs very little movement to work the controls and may even be voice-controlled.

Large computer systems will still exist in colleges, universities and research centres, but microcomputers are being used in more and more of the offices and laboratories to deal with the smaller problems.

Microcomputers are often found in laboratories. They are used as an aid to research work. The picture above shows how easily a micro-computer fits in. It is no bigger than a portable electric typewriter, and is readily available to the scientist.

Above: Learning to spell is much more fun when you can do it this way. The computer speaks a word to you and you have to spell it. If you get it wrong, the computer will soon tell you!

Left: This equipment helps handicapped children who cannot speak and who have very little hand or arm movement. By using a switch, the child is able to 'point' to a picture by moving the light at the back of the screen.

Right: These children in a classroom are watching a television screen. This television screen is linked to a computer.

# Computers in everyday life

Both large and small computers are useful in business and industry. In many big companies, much of the everyday work is done by a computer. It is, for example, extremely useful for doing all the calculations which are necessary to work out wages. It is quick and accurate, and can also print out all the information for the employee.

Many other everyday business tasks can also be done on a computer. For example, information can be given to the computer on the amount of stock available in the shop or store room. The computer can list those items, which need to be ordered. This stock control could be done by microcomputers, which are small enough to hold in your hand. They could be carried round the shelves to record the amount of stock. This information could then be sent to a central computer, which would sort out the information from a number of different microcomputers, and keep a central record of stock.

The picture above shows a computer room that you might find in any large company. Three computer operators can be seen – the one in the centre is controlling what the computer is doing, while the other two operators check that all is working correctly.

There are jobs which secretaries and clerks do which can easily be done by computer. Many offices now have a machine called a 'Word Processor' which is used for printing out letters and documents. Word Processors can store everything they produce in the 'memory', so corrections can easily be made without retyping the whole of a document. Computer systems which deal with such tasks as sorting mail, keeping a diary and circulating information, are now being brought into the office.

Telex, the electronic method of sending letters and documents from one office to another, is already very popular. Pictures can now be sent electronically as well and it does not make any difference if they are being sent from one office to another in the same city, or to one in a different country.

Computers are also important for controlling traffic on our roads. Traffic lights are probably the best known example. The police can watch the traffic in some places by using television cameras which have been placed high above street level.

This policeman at the Scotland Yard traffic control centre is watching the flow of traffic on screens.

## IN THE OFFICE

You can see from these two pictures how offices have changed in the last hundred years. In the past there were many clerks and office staff working long hours and writing everything by hand. Now, as shown in the picture on the right, a computer has taken over much of the routine work. Only a few people are needed to operate it.

Computers and electronics have made an impact on travel: we have already seen how they make air travel safer. Flights are booked through computers, and travel agents use terminals connected to a central computer to book holidays. Ships also make use of computers. They can be a help to navigation, and are also used to control the movement of the ship.

The movement of freight by rail is often controlled and checked by a central computer system. In this way, the best possible use can be made of the wagons and locomotives, and they can be kept moving.

Weather-forecasting is now done with the use of computers. More accurate forecasting can help make travel safer and is of great use to farmers and sailors in particular.

This is a computer system used in medicine. Computers can be used to help in the detection of disease, and can store and analyse information.

Another important use of computers is in medicine. Computers, both large and small, are of course used for medical research. But computers and electronics also play a part in the everyday life of the hospital. They are used in machines that check the health of different parts of the body, as well as in X-ray machines and body-scanners which help detect diseases. Computer systems have also been developed which ask patients the kind of questions normally asked by your doctor. The answers can then be considered later by the doctor.

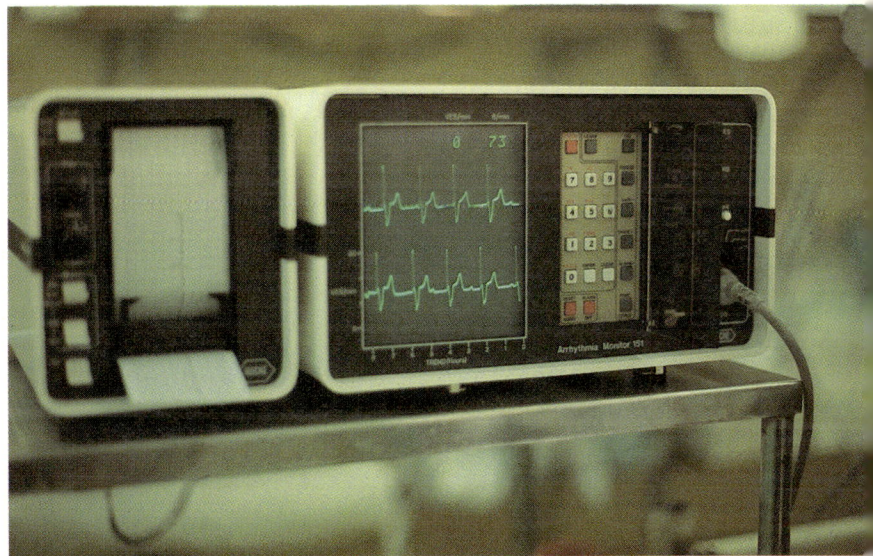

## RAILWAYS

When a train is running at night, its movement is checked and controlled by a computer in order to make sure it arrives safely and on time. On the left is a picture of British Rail's computer system. You can see the disc units which are used to store hundreds of items of information about the movement of trains, and any problems which might mean a delay in their journey.

25

# Control in the factory

Many everyday jobs in the factory, which need very accurate measurement or movement, can best be done by equipment which is controlled by a computer. Jobs that require very high precision can be done more quickly and more efficiently by computer-controlled machine-tools.

In a production line, the goods being manufactured pass through different stages. The production process can be controlled by a computer, and few people, if any, are required. Each stage of production can also be separately controlled. Information is passed from the computer to the production control computer, which makes sure that everything is running smoothly.

Right: The inside of a British Steel factory. The picture shows red-hot steel being lifted from the furnace. The equipment is controlled by a computer.

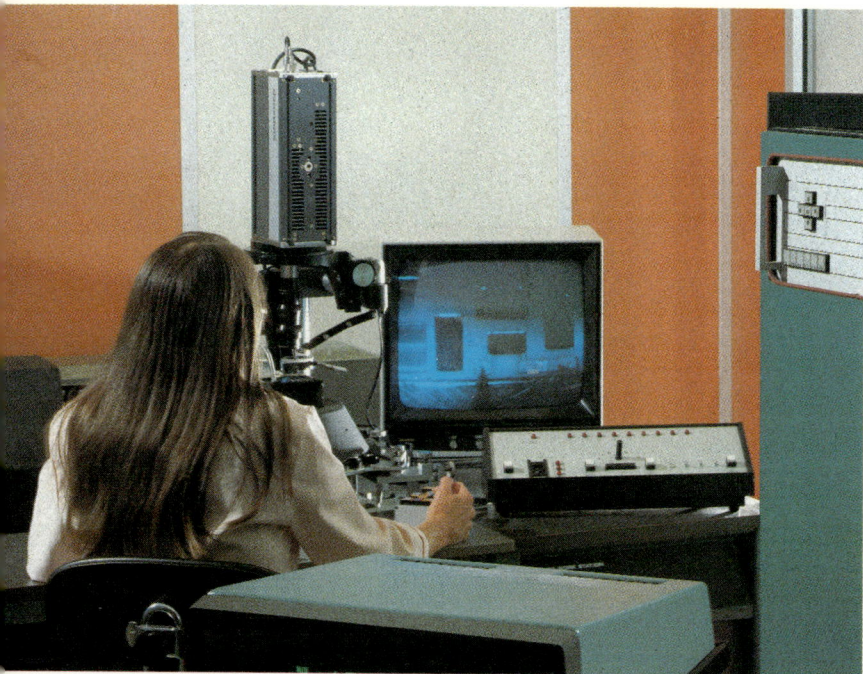

Left: Computers are used for tasks which require high precision and accuracy. Here, you can see the trimming of microprocessors by a computer-controlled laser beam.

There are many jobs which used to be done by people in such places as factories, mines and mills, which were difficult or dangerous to do. These jobs can now be carried out safely by computer-controlled equipment. This results in better working conditions for those people who are involved in such work. In fact, computer-controlled equipment can be used to work in conditions in which people would not want to work.

The influence of computers can be noticed even before you get far inside the factory or workplace. When each worker 'clocks in' or 'clocks out', the information is stored and used by a computer to work out his wages and overtime pay.

Above: This is an important item of equipment in the factory. This machine is used by employees to 'clock in' and 'clock out'.

# Robots

Robots are a form of computer-controlled equipment. Most people think of robots as mechanical human beings. Or they think they look like the robots in science fiction films. However, at present, robots are mostly used to do routine tasks on production lines and, instead of looking human, they look more like mechanical arms.

These robots can do complicated movements with great precision under the control of a microcomputer. They will play an ever more important part in the factories of tomorrow by helping towards cheaper production – robots can work 24 hours a day and do not need to take time off to eat or sleep!

Below: This is an example of a robot being used in industry. Robots are used to do monotonous jobs, and often work in places where it is dangerous or even impossible for a human being to work.

Above: This is the production line in a car factory. Robots are being used to help put the car together. It is one example of how robots can relieve factory workers of repetitive, routine tasks.

Left: Many people will imagine robots to be like R2–D2 and C–3PO who appeared in the film *Star Wars*. Of course these two friendly robots are simply the result of someone's imagination – but who can say what will happen to robots in the future?

# Glimpses of the future

It is difficult to know just how computers and electronics will change our lives. One thing is certain: computers will play a very important role for a long time to come. For instance, as the amount of space travel increases, so will the need for better computers to navigate and control spaceships.

At home, computers will make everyday tasks much easier. Perhaps every home will have a 'robot servant' – just give it the orders for the day and forget the household chores! As computers take over jobs at home and at work, there will be far more free time for people to do what they want. There will also be fewer jobs, which may create problems. Perhaps computers themselves can help solve these problems.

Spacecraft need computers to record information and send it back to Earth. A signal to Earth from a spacecraft near Jupiter can take up to 51 minutes.

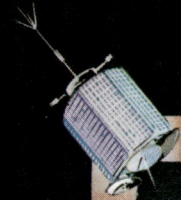

When you call someone on the telephone, you will be able to see them as well as speak to them – so remember to look your best. They can see you!

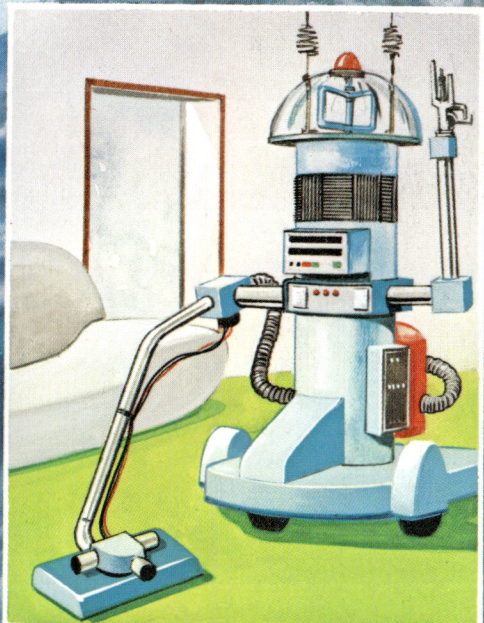

Is this your servant of the future? Will there be one in every home, and what will be its duties? Maybe it will be able to detect any faults and even repair itself!

# Glossary

**Calculator**
A machine designed to do basic arithmetic (addition, subtraction, multiplication, division) and other more complicated activities.

**Computer**
Electronic equipment which is able to send and receive information, to store and to act upon such information by carrying out a set of instructions. A computer may be used to do calculations or to control other equipment.

**Digital**
Information which is presented in terms of a number is said to be in digital form.

**Dopant**
A chemical element which combines with the silicon during the making of a 'chip'.

**Electron**
A particle which makes it possible to pass electricity through certain materials.

**Electronics**
The study of the movement of electrons.

**Input**
Information received by a computer.

**Integrated circuit**
Many components linked together on a single unit.

**Multi-user system**
A computer system which can be used by more than one person at the same time.

**Output**
Information sent out by a computer.

**Program**
The set of instructions given to a computer.

**Robot**
A machine able to do work without supervision. It is often controlled by a computer.

**Silicon chip**
A small wafer of silicon containing one or more integrated circuit.

**Transistor**
A small piece of electronics capable of controlling the movement of electrons, like a valve. However, it is much smaller and stronger than a valve, and uses less power.

**Valve**
Used to control the movement of electrons, and thus the electrical current, through a circuit.

**VDU**
Visual Display Unit, attached to a computer and used to communicate with the computer. Information passing between the person using the VDU and the computer is shown on a screen similar to a television.

**Word processor**
An advanced kind of typewriter used to produce and store letters and documents. Errors can be corrected without retyping the whole of the material.

Today, smaller and smaller chips are being manufactured, as you can see in this picture.

# Index